THE BRANCH WILL NOT BREAK

THE BRANCH
WILL NOT BREAK

POEMS BY

JAMES WRIGHT

Ach, könt' ich dorthin kommen,
Und dort mein Herz erfreu'n,
Und aller Qual entnommen,
Und frei und selig sein.

Ach, jedes Land der Wonne!
Das seh' ich oft im Traum.
Doch kommt die Morgensonne,
Zerfliesst's wie eitel Schaum.

WESLEYAN UNIVERSITY PRESS
MIDDLETOWN, CONNECTICUT

For permission to reprint some of these poems, the author wishes to make due acknowledgment to the editors of the following: *The Fifties, The Sixties, The Minnesota Review, Big Table, Harper's Magazine, The Paris Review, Audience, Botteghe Oscure, Poetry* (Chicago), *The Kenyon Review, The New York Times* (daily), *The Nation, Chicago Choice,* and *The Hudson Review.* The poem "By a Lake in Minnesota" appeared originally in *The New Yorker.*

I am also grateful to three particular friends: Miss Mary Bly, for her self and for the poem which bears her name; Heinrich Heine, for his beautiful song "Aus alten Märchen winkt es"; and Allen Tate, for his friendship in a difficult time.

All inquiries and permissions requests should be addressed to the Publisher, Wesleyan University Press, 110 Mt. Vernon Street, Middletown, Connecticut 06457

Distributed by Harper & Row Publishers, Keystone Industrial Park, Scranton, Pennsylvania 18512

Manufactured in the United States of America
First printing, 1963; tenth printing, 1983

ELEUTHERIA

Μνάσεσθαί τινά φαιμ᾽ ὑστερον ἀμμέοιν.

(Sappho)

CONTENTS

THE BRANCH WILL NOT BREAK

AS I STEP OVER A PUDDLE AT THE END OF WINTER, I THINK OF AN ANCIENT CHINESE GOVERNOR

And how can I, born in evil days
And fresh from failure, ask a kindness
of Fate?
— Written A.D. 819

Po Chu-i, balding old politician,
What's the use?
I think of you,
Uneasily entering the gorges of the Yang-Tze,
When you were being towed up the rapids
Toward some political job or other
In the city of Chungshou.
You made it, I guess,
By dark.

But it is 1960, it is almost spring again,
And the tall rocks of Minneapolis
Build me my own black twilight
Of bamboo ropes and waters.
Where is Yuan Chen, the friend you loved?
Where is the sea, that once solved the whole loneliness
Of the Midwest? Where is Minneapolis? I can see nothing
But the great terrible oak tree darkening with winter.
Did you find the city of isolated men beyond mountains?
Or have you been holding the end of a frayed rope
For a thousand years?

GOODBYE TO THE POETRY OF CALCIUM

Dark cypresses—
The world is uneasily happy:
It will all be forgotten.
                    —THEODOR STORM

Mother of roots, you have not seeded
The tall ashes of loneliness
For me. Therefore,
Now I go.
If I knew the name,
Your name, all trellises of vineyards and old fire
Would quicken to shake terribly my
Earth, mother of spiralling searches, terrible
Fable of calcium, girl. I crept this afternoon
In weeds once more,
Casual, daydreaming you might not strike
Me down. Mother of window sills and journeys,
Hallower of scratching hands,
The sight of my blind man makes me want to weep.
Tiller of waves or whatever, woman or man,
Mother of roots or father of diamonds,
Look: I am nothing.
I do not even have ashes to rub into my eyes.

IN FEAR OF HARVESTS

It has happened
Before: nearby,
The nostrils of slow horses
Breathe evenly,
And the brown bees drag their high garlands,
Heavily,
Toward hives of snow.

THREE STANZAS FROM GOETHE

That man standing there, who is he?
His path lost in the thicket,
Behind him the bushes
Lash back together,
The grass rises again,
The waste devours him.

Oh, who will heal the sufferings
Of the man whose balm turned poison?
Who drank nothing
But hatred of men from love's abundance?
Once despised, now a despiser,
He kills his own life,
The precious secret.
The self-seeker finds nothing.

Oh Father of Love,
If your psaltery holds one tone
That his ear still might echo,
Then quicken his heart!
Open his eyes, shut off by clouds
From the thousand fountains
So near him, dying of thirst
In his own desert.

(NOTE: These three stanzas are from
Goethe's poem "Harzreise im Winter."
They are the stanzas which Brahms
detached from the poem and em-
ployed as the text for his "Alto
Rhapsody" of 1869.)

AUTUMN BEGINS IN MARTINS FERRY, OHIO

In the Shreve High football stadium,
I think of Polacks nursing long beers in Tiltonsville,
And gray faces of Negroes in the blast furnace at Benwood,
And the ruptured night watchman of Wheeling Steel,
Dreaming of heroes.

All the proud fathers are ashamed to go home.
Their women cluck like starved pullets,
Dying for love.

Therefore,
Their sons grow suicidally beautiful
At the beginning of October,
And gallop terribly against each other's bodies.

LYING IN A HAMMOCK AT WILLIAM DUFFY'S
FARM IN PINE ISLAND, MINNESOTA

Over my head, I see the bronze butterfly,
Asleep on the black trunk,
Blowing like a leaf in green shadow.
Down the ravine behind the empty house,
The cowbells follow one another
Into the distances of the afternoon.
To my right,
In a field of sunlight between two pines,
The droppings of last year's horses
Blaze up into golden stones.
I lean back, as the evening darkens and comes on.
A chicken hawk floats over, looking for home.
I have wasted my life.

THE JEWEL

There is this cave
In the air behind my body
That nobody is going to touch:
A cloister, a silence
Closing around a blossom of fire.
When I stand upright in the wind,
My bones turn to dark emeralds.

IN THE FACE OF HATRED

I am frightened by the sorrow
Of escaping animals.
The snake moves slowly
Beyond his horizon of yellow stone.
A great harvest of convicts has shaken loose
And hurries across the wall of your eyes.
Most of them, all moving alike,
Are gone already along the river.
Only two boys,
Trailed by shadows of rooted police,
Turn aimlessly in the lashing elderberries.
One cries for his father's death,
And the other, the silent one,
Listens into the hallway
Of a dark leaf.

FEAR IS WHAT QUICKENS ME

1.

Many animals that our fathers killed in America
Had quick eyes.
They stared about wildly,
When the moon went dark.
The new moon falls into the freight yards
Of cities in the south,
But the loss of the moon to the dark hands of Chicago
Does not matter to the deer
In this northern field.

2.

What is that tall woman doing
There, in the trees?
I can hear rabbits and mourning doves whispering together
In the dark grass, there
Under the trees.

3.

I look about wildly.

A MESSAGE HIDDEN IN AN EMPTY WINE BOTTLE THAT I THREW INTO A GULLY OF MAPLE TREES ONE NIGHT AT AN INDECENT HOUR

Women are dancing around a fire
By a pond of creosote and waste water from the river
In the dank fog of Ohio.
They are dead.
I am alone here,
And I reach for the moon that dangles
Cold on a dark vine.
The unwashed shadows
Of blast furnaces from Moundsville, West Virginia,
Are sneaking across the pits of strip mines
To steal grapes
In heaven.
Nobody else knows I am here.
All right.
Come out, come out, I am dying.
I am growing old.
An owl rises
From the cutter bar
Of a hayrake.

STAGES ON A JOURNEY WESTWARD

1.

I began in Ohio.
I still dream of home.
Near Mansfield, enormous dobbins enter dark barns in
    autumn,
Where they can be lazy, where they can munch little apples,
Or sleep long.
But by night now, in the bread lines my father
Prowls, I cannot find him: So far off,
1500 miles or so away, and yet
I can hardy sleep.
In a blue rag the old man limps to my bed,
Leading a blind horse
Of gentleness.
In 1932, grimy with machinery, he sang me
A lullaby of a goosegirl.
Outside the house, the slag heaps waited.

2.

In western Minnesota, just now,
I slept again.
In my dream, I crouched over a fire.
The only human beings between me and the Pacific Ocean
Were old Indians, who wanted to kill me.
They squat and stare for hours into small fires
Far off in the mountains.
The blades of their hatchets are dirty with the grease
Of huge, silent buffaloes.

3.

It is dawn.
I am shivering,
Even beneath a huge eiderdown.
I came in last night, drunk,
And left the oil stove cold.
I listen a long time, now, to the flurries.
Snow howls all around me, out of the abandoned prairies.
It sounds like the voices of bums and gamblers,
Rattling through the bare nineteenth-century whorehouses
In Nevada.

4.

Defeated for re-election,
The half-educated sheriff of Mukilteo, Washington,
Has been drinking again.
He leads me up the cliff, tottering.
Both drunk, we stand among the graves.
Miners paused here on the way up to Alaska.
Angry, they spaded their broken women's bodies
Into ditches of crab grass.
I lie down between tombstones.
At the bottom of the cliff
America is over and done with.
America,
Plunged into the dark furrows
Of the sea again.

HOW MY FEVER LEFT

I can still hear her.
She hobbles downstairs to the kitchen.
She is swearing at the dishes.
She slaps her grease rags
Into a basket,
And slings it over her skinny forearm, crooked
With hatred, and stomps outside.
I can hear my father downstairs,
Standing without a coat in the open back door,
Calling to the old bat across the snow.
She's forgotten her black shawl,
But I see her through my window, sneering,
Flapping upward
Toward some dark church on the hill.
She has to meet somebody else, and
It's no use, she won't listen,
She's gone.

MINERS

1.

The police are probing tonight for the bodies
Of children in the black waters
Of the suburbs.

2.

Below the chemical riffles of the Ohio River,
Grappling hooks
Drag delicately about, between skiff hulks and sand shoals,
Until they clasp
Fingers.

3.

Somewhere in a vein of Bridgeport, Ohio;
Deep in a coal hill behind Hanna's name;
Below the tipples, and dark as a drowsy woodchuck;
A man, alone,
Stumbles upon the outside locks of a grave, whispering
Oh let me in.

4.

Many American women mount long stairs
In the shafts of houses,
Fall asleep, and emerge suddenly into tottering palaces.

IN OHIO

White mares lashed to the sulky carriages
Trot softly
Around the dismantled fairgrounds
Near Buckeye Lake.

The sandstone blocks of a wellspring
Cool dark green moss.

The sun floats down, a small golden lemon dissolves
In the water.
I dream, as I lean over the edge, of a crawdad's mouth.

The cellars of haunted houses are like ancient cities,
Fallen behind a big heap of apples.

A widow on a front porch puckers her lips
And whispers.

TWO POEMS ABOUT PRESIDENT HARDING

ONE: *His Death*

In Marion, the honey locust trees are falling.
Everybody in town remembers the white hair,
The campaign of a lost summer, the front porch
Open to the public, and the vaguely stunned smile
Of a lucky man.

"Neighbor, I want to be helpful," he said once.
Later, "You think I'm honest, don't you?"
Weeping drunk.

I am drunk this evening in 1961,
In a jag for my countryman,
Who died of crab meat on the way back from Alaska.
Everyone knows that joke.

How many honey locusts have fallen,
Pitched rootlong into the open graves of strip mines,
Since the First World War ended
And Wilson the gaunt deacon jogged sullenly
Into silence?
Tonight,
The cancerous ghosts of old con men
Shed their leaves.
For a proud man,
Lost between the turnpike near Cleveland
And the chiropractors' signs looming among dead mul-
    berry trees,
There is no place left to go
But home.

"Warren lacks mentality," one of his friends said.

Yet he was beautiful, he was the snowfall
Turned to white stallions standing still
Under dark elm trees.

He died in public. He claimed the secret right
To be ashamed.

Two: *His Tomb in Ohio*

"... he died of a busted gut."
—MENCKEN, on BRYAN.

A hundred slag piles north of us,
At the mercy of the moon and rain,
He lies in his ridiculous
Tomb, our fellow citizen.
No, I have never seen that place,
Where many shadows of faceless thieves
Chuckle and stumble and embrace
On beer cans, stogie butts, and graves.

One holiday, one rainy week
After the country fell apart,
Hoover and Coolidge came to speak
And snivel about his broken heart.
His grave, a huge absurdity,
Embarrassed cops and visitors.
Hoover and Coolidge crept away
By night, and women closed their doors.

Now junkmen call their children in
Before they catch their death of cold;
Young lovers let the moon begin
Its quick spring; and the day grows old;

27

The mean one-legger who rakes up leaves
Has chased the loafers out of the park;
Minnegan Leonard half-believes
In God, and the poolroom goes dark;

America goes on, goes on
Laughing, and Harding was a fool.
Even his big pretentious stone
Lays him bare to ridicule.
I know it. But don't look at me.
By God, I didn't start this mess.
Whatever moon and rain may be,
The hearts of men are merciless.

EISENHOWER'S VISIT TO FRANCO, 1959

> "... we die of cold, and not of darkness."
> —UNAMUNO

The American hero must triumph over
The forces of darkness.
He has flown through the very light of heaven
And come down in the slow dusk
Of Spain.

Franco stands in a shining circle of police.
His arms open in welcome.
He promises all dark things
Will be hunted down.

State police yawn in the prisons.
Antonio Machado follows the moon
Down a road of white dust,
To a cave of silent children
Under the Pyrenees.
Wine darkens in stone jars in villages.
Wine sleeps in the mouths of old men, it is a dark red
    color.

Smiles glitter in Madrid.
Eisenhower has touched hands with Franco, embracing
In a glare of photographers.
Clean new bombers from America muffle their engines
And glide down now.

Their wings shine in the searchlights
Of bare fields,
In Spain.

IN MEMORY OF A SPANISH POET

> *Take leave of the sun, and of the*
> *wheat, for me.*
> —MIGUEL HERNANDEZ,
> written in prison, 1942.

I see you strangling
Under the black ripples of whitewashed walls.
Your hands turn yellow in the ruins of the sun.
I dream of your slow voice, flying,
Planting the dark waters of the spirit
With lutes and seeds.

Here, in the American Midwest,
Those seeds fly out of the field and across the strange
     heaven of my skull.
They scatter out of their wings a quiet farewell,
A greeting to my country.

Now twilight gathers,
A long sundown.
Silos creep away toward the west.

THE UNDERMINING OF THE DEFENSE ECONOMY

Stairway, face, window,
Mottled animals
Running over the public buildings.
Maple and elm.
In the autumn
Of early evening,
A pumpkin
Lies on its side,
Turning yellow as the face
Of a discharged general.
It's no use complaining, the economy
Is going to hell with all these radical
Changes,
Girls the color of butterflies
That can't be sold.
Only after nightfall,
Little boys lie still, awake,
Wondering, wondering,
Delicate little boxes of dust.

TWILIGHTS

The big stones of the cistern behind the barn
Are soaked in whitewash.
My grandmother's face is a small maple leaf
Pressed in a secret box.
Locusts are climbing down into the dark green crevices
Of my childhood. Latches click softly in the trees. Your hair
    is gray.

The arbors of the cities are withered.
Far off, the shopping centers empty and darken.

A red shadow of steel mills.

Number One

I slouch in bed.
Beyond the streaked trees of my window,
All groves are bare.
Locusts and poplars change to unmarried women
Sorting slate from anthracite
Between railroad ties:
The yellow-bearded winter of the depression
Is still alive somewhere, an old man
Counting his collection of bottle caps
In a tarpaper shack under the cold trees
Of my grave.

I still feel half drunk,
And all those old women beyond my window
Are hunching toward the graveyard.

Drunk, mumbling Hungarian,
The sun staggers in,
And his big stupid face pitches
Into the stove.
For two hours I have been dreaming
Of green butterflies searching for diamonds
In coal seams;
And children chasing each other for a game
Through the hills of fresh graves.
But the sun has come home drunk from the sea,

And a sparrow outside
Sings of the Hanna Coal Co. and the dead moon.
The filaments of cold light bulbs tremble
In music like delicate birds.
Ah, turn it off.

NUMBER TWO: I TRY TO WAKEN AND GREET THE WORLD
ONCE AGAIN

In a pine tree,
A few yards away from my window sill,
A brilliant blue jay is springing up and down, up and
down,
On a branch.
I laugh, as I see him abandon himself
To entire delight, for he knows as well as I do
That the branch will not break.

DEPRESSED BY A BOOK OF BAD POETRY, I WALK TOWARD AN UNUSED PASTURE AND INVITE THE INSECTS TO JOIN ME

Relieved, I let the book fall behind a stone.
I climb a slight rise of grass.
I do not want to disturb the ants
Who are walking single file up the fence post,
Carrying small white petals,
Casting shadows so frail that I can see through them.
I close my eyes for a moment, and listen.
The old grasshoppers
Are tired, they leap heavily now,
Their thighs are burdened.
I want to hear them, they have clear sounds to make.
Then lovely, far off, a dark cricket begins
In the maple trees.

TWO HORSES PLAYING IN THE ORCHARD

Too soon, too soon, a man will come
To lock the gate, and drive them home.
Then, neighing softly through the night,
The mare will nurse her shoulder bite.
Now, lightly fair, through lock and mane
She gazes over the dusk again,
And sees her darkening stallion leap
In grass for apples, half asleep.

Lightly, lightly, on slender knees
He turns, lost in a dream of trees.
Apples are slow to find this day,
Someone has stolen the best away.
Still, some remain before the snow,
A few, trembling on boughs so low
A horse can reach them, small and sweet:
And some are tumbling to her feet.

Too soon, a man will scatter them,
Although I do not know his name,
His age, or how he came to own
A horse, an apple tree, a stone.
I let those horses in to steal
On principle, because I feel
Like half a horse myself, although
Too soon, too soon, already. Now.

BY A LAKE IN MINNESOTA

Upshore from the cloud—
The slow whale of country twilight—
The spume of light falls into valleys
Full of roses.

And below,
Out of the placid waters,
Two beavers, mother and child,
Wave out long ripples
To the dust of dead leaves
On the shore.

And the moon walks,
Hunting for hidden dolphins
Behind the darkening combers
Of the ground.

And downshore from the cloud,
I stand, waiting
For dark.

BEGINNING

The moon drops one or two feathers into the field.
The dark wheat listens.
Be still.
Now.
There they are, the moon's young, trying
Their wings.
Between trees, a slender woman lifts up the lovely shadow
Of her face, and now she steps into the air, now she is gone
Wholly, into the air.
I stand alone by an elder tree, I do not dare breathe
Or move.
I listen.
The wheat leans back toward its own darkness,
And I lean toward mine.

FROM A BUS WINDOW IN CENTRAL OHIO,
JUST BEFORE A THUNDER SHOWER

Cribs loaded with roughage huddle together
Before the north clouds.
The wind tiptoes between poplars.
The silver maple leaves squint
Toward the ground.
An old farmer, his scarlet face
Apologetic with whiskey, swings back a barn door
And calls a hundred black-and-white Holsteins
From the clover field.

MARCH

A bear under the snow
Turns over to yawn.
It's been a long, hard rest.

Once, as she lay asleep, her cubs fell
Out of her hair,
And she did not know them.

It is hard to breathe
In a tight grave:

So she roars,
And the roof breaks.
Dark rivers and leaves
Pour down.

When the wind opens its doors
In its own good time,
The cubs follow that relaxed and beautiful
    woman
Outside to the unfamiliar cities
Of moss.

TRYING TO PRAY

This time, I have left my body behind me, crying
In its dark thorns.
Still,
There are good things in this world.
It is dusk.
It is the good darkness
Of women's hands that touch loaves.
The spirit of a tree begins to move.
I touch leaves.
I close my eyes, and think of water.

TWO SPRING CHARMS

fragments from the Norwegian

1.

Now it is late winter.

Years ago,
I walked through a spring wind
Bending green wheat
In a field near Trondhjem.

2.

Black snow,
Like a strange sea creature,
Draws back into itself,
Restoring grass to earth.

SPRING IMAGES

Two athletes
Are dancing in the cathedral
Of the wind.

A butterfly lights on the branch
Of your green voice.

Small antelopes
Fall asleep in the ashes
Of the moon.

ARRIVING IN THE COUNTRY AGAIN

The white house is silent.
My friends can't hear me yet.
The flicker who lives in the bare tree at the
field's edge
Pecks once and is still for a long time.
I stand still in the late afternoon.
My face is turned away from the sun.
A horse grazes in my long shadow.

IN THE COLD HOUSE

I slept a few minutes ago,
Even though the stove has been out for hours.
I am growing old.
A bird cries in bare elder trees.

SNOWSTORM IN THE MIDWEST

Though haunches of whales
Slope into whitecap doves,
It is hard to drown here.

Between two walls,
A fold of echoes,
A girl's voice walks naked.

I step into the water
Of two flakes.
The crowns of white birds rise
To my ankles,
To my knees,
To my face.

Escaping in silence
From locomotive and smoke,
I hunt the huge feathers of gulls
And the fountains of hills,
I hunt the sea, to walk on the waters.

A splayed starling
Follows me down a long stairway
Of white sand.

HAVING LOST MY SONS, I CONFRONT THE WRECKAGE OF THE MOON: CHRISTMAS, 1960

After dark
Near the South Dakota border,
The moon is out hunting, everywhere,
Delivering fire,
And walking down hallways
Of a diamond.

Behind a tree,
It lights on the ruins
Of a white city:
Frost, frost.

Where are they gone,
Who lived there?

Bundled away under wings
And dark faces.

I am sick
Of it, and I go on,
Living, alone, alone,
Past the charred silos, past the hidden graves
Of Chippewas and Norwegians.

This cold winter
Moon spills the inhuman fire
Of jewels
Into my hands.

Dead riches, dead hands, the moon
Darkens,
And I am lost in the beautiful white ruins
Of America.

AMERICAN WEDDING

She dreamed long of waters.
Inland today, she wakens
On scraped knees, lost
Among locust thorns.

She gropes for
The path backward, to
The pillows of the sea.

Bruised trillium
Of wilderness, she
May rest on briar leaves,
As long as the wind cares to pause.

Now she is going to learn
How it is that animals
Can save time:
They sleep a whole season
Of lamentation and snow,
Without bothering to weep.

A PRAYER TO ESCAPE FROM THE MARKET PLACE

I renounce the blindness of the magazines.
I want to lie down under a tree.
This is the only duty that is not death.
This is the everlasting happiness
Of small winds.
Suddenly,
A pheasant flutters, and I turn
Only to see him vanishing at the damp edge
Of the road.

RAIN

It is the sinking of things.

Flashlights drift over dark trees,
Girls kneel,
An owl's eyelids fall.

The sad bones of my hands descend into a valley
Of strange rocks.

TODAY I WAS SO HAPPY, SO I MADE THIS POEM

As the plump squirrel scampers
Across the roof of the corncrib,
The moon suddenly stands up in the darkness,
And I see that it is impossible to die.
Each moment of time is a mountain.
An eagle rejoices in the oak trees of heaven,
Crying
This is what I wanted.

MARY BLY

I sit here, doing nothing, alone, worn out by long winter.
I feel the light breath of the newborn child.
Her face is smooth as the side of an apricot,
Eyes quick as her blond mother's hands.
She has full, soft, red hair, and as she lies quiet
In her tall mother's arms, her delicate hands
Weave back and forth.
I feel the seasons changing beneath me,
Under the floor.
She is braiding the waters of air into the plaited manes
Of happy colts.
They canter, without making a sound, along the shores
Of melting snow.

TO THE EVENING STAR: CENTRAL MINNESOTA

Under the water tower at the edge of town
A huge Airedale ponders a long ripple
In the grass fields beyond.
Miles off, a whole grove silently
Flies up into the darkness.
One light comes on in the sky,
One lamp on the prairie.

Beautiful daylight of the body, your hands carry seashells.
West of this wide plain,
Animals wilder than ours
Come down from the green mountains in the darkness.
Now they can see you, they know
The open meadows are safe.

I WAS AFRAID OF DYING

Once,
I was afraid of dying
In a field of dry weeds.
But now,
All day long I have been walking among damp fields,
Trying to keep still, listening
To insects that move patiently.
Perhaps they are sampling the fresh dew that gathers slowly
In empty snail shells
And in the secret shelters of sparrow feathers fallen on the
    earth.

A BLESSING

Just off the highway to Rochester, Minnesota,
Twilight bounds softly forth on the grass.
And the eyes of those two Indian ponies
Darken with kindness.
They have come gladly out of the willows
To welcome my friend and me.
We step over the barbed wire into the pasture
Where they have been grazing all day, alone.
They ripple tensely, they can hardly contain their
        happiness
That we have come.
They bow shyly as wet swans. They love each other.
There is no loneliness like theirs.
At home once more,
They begin munching the young tufts of spring in the
        darkness.
I would like to hold the slenderer one in my arms,
For she has walked over to me
And nuzzled my left hand.
She is black and white,
Her mane falls wild on her forehead,
And the light breeze moves me to caress her long ear
That is delicate as the skin over a girl's wrist.
Suddenly I realize
That if I stepped out of my body I would break
Into blossom.

MILKWEED

While I stood here, in the open, lost in myself,
I must have looked a long time
Down the corn rows, beyond grass,
The small house,
White walls, animals lumbering toward the barn.
I look down now. It is all changed.
Whatever it was I lost, whatever I wept for
Was a wild, gentle thing, the small dark eyes
Loving me in secret.
It is here. At a touch of my hand,
The air fills with delicate creatures
From the other world.

A DREAM OF BURIAL

Nothing was left of me
But my right foot
And my left shoulder.
They lay white as the skein of a spider floating
In a field of snow toward a dark building
Tilted and stained by wind.
Inside the dream, I dreamed on.

A parade of old women
Sang softly above me,
Faint mosquitoes near still water.

So I waited, in my corridor.
I listened for the sea
To call me.
I knew that, somewhere outside, the horse
Stood saddled, browsing in grass,
Waiting for me.